عبد الرحمة

Book One

Let's
Read & Write
Arabic

Fadel Abdallah

 IQRA' International Educational Foundation

Part of a Comprehensive and Systematic Program of Islamic Studies

Program of Arabic Studies

Read and Write Arabic
Elementary Level - All Beginners

First in a series of two books.

Chief Program Editors:

Abidullah al-Ansari Ghazi
Ph.D. History of Religion, Harvard

Tasneema Khatoon Ghazi
Ph.D. Curriculum and Reading,
University of Minnesota

Reviewers:

Assad N. Busool
Prof. of Arabic at AIC, Chicago

Khalil Tahrawi
Instructor of Arabic at
Saudi Islamic Academy,
Washington D.C.

Design:

Aliuddin Khaja

IQRA' International Educational Foundation,
7450 Skokie Blvd., Skokie, IL 60077
Tel: 847-673-4072; Fax: 847-673-4095
email: iqra@aol.com
website: www.iqra.org

ISBN # 1-56316-005-6

Table of Contents

INTRODUCTION

Within IQRA' Systematic and Comprehensive Program of Arabic and Qur'anic Studies, two activity books have been published and have been widely used in the schools that teach Arabic. In **Sail Through with Arabic Letters**, the individual letters of the Arabic Alphabet were introduced in isolated forms, so that the pre-school learners will get initial familiarization with the basic forms of the letters when they stand alone. Associated with each letter, one actual word was introduced in which the letter appears at the beginning of it.

This basic step was carried on further in **Shapes and Forms of Arabic Letters**, where the letters of the alphabet were introduced in their different shapes; at the beginning, middle and final positions of the words.

However, many of the 84 words introduced in the above cited books are not words that occurred in the Qur'an. They were selected rather for being easy to illustrate in picture form, so that the meaning could be conveyed through the visual effect.

To bring the younger learner a step closer to the pronunciation and writing of the Arabic language of the Qur'an, the present activity book was conceived. Its idea focuses on using frequently repeated words of the Qur'an as the basis for further practicing activities in pronunciation, reading and writing Arabic.

In this way this book can both be used in conjunction with Arabic language classes as well as with Qur'anic classes, at a higher level of learning; say first to third grades students or adult learners who have already learned their Arabic Alphabet and have a leaning to concentrate on the Arabic language of the Qur'an.

To achieve the intended purpose of this activity book, illustrations were disregarded for two reasons; first, not all words can actually be illustrated; second, illustrations will be done at the expense of the space we need to devote for writing. To compensate for illustrations to convey the meaning, the English meaning of the words were given at the bottom of each lesson.

As to the format of the present book, it consists of two parts. Part 1 is intended to be a **preliminary review of the Arabic letters and their forms and shapes, along with the varied pronunciations in combination with**

short and long vowels. Through this section, the learners will be introduced to 84 key Qur'anic words; most of them would be new words the learners and did not encounter in the previous two books cited above.

Part 2 contains selected Qur'anic words, in alphabetical order, used with high frequency in the Qur'an. Representing each letter of the Arabic Alphabet, there are four words containing that letter. However, there is an exception with the *"Hamzah"*; there are four words representing *"Hamzat-ul-Madd"* and another four words representing *"Hamzat-ul-Qat'"*

Starting with lesson eleven and running through lesson thirty-five, there is an extra line on top of each page introducing the individual Arabic letter in nine sound variations for each. This part is intended for oral practice only, before the students are introduced to the pronunciation and writing of the actual words. Covering this section is very important since it will greatly help the learners to master the main variations of sounds at an early stage. It is recommended that the teacher will articulate each of these nine sound variations aloud, for at least three times each, asking the students to repeat after her or him.

To help the student read the word he or she is writing, especially at home with non-Arabic speaking parents, a transliteration of each word was provided in parenthesis as an aid for special linguistic group. When the work is done in a class setting, under the direct supervision of a native teacher of the language, then this transliteration should be discarded.

Teachers who used this book before will notice that this is a new expanded and **improved edition** of the original work. And by the time learners have covered this book, they would have learned approximately 250 key Qur'anic words; both pronunciation and writing.

Finally, this reading-writing activity book should suit the learning needs of 1st and 2nd grades learners who have already covered IQRA's two other books: **Sail Through with Arabic Letters and Shapes** and **Forms of Arabic Letters** during previous stages of learning Arabic.
The present book is followed by another higher level book 2, based on the same concept and approach for 3rd and 4th graders.

Fadel Abdallah,
Chicago, *Jumada* I 1426 / June 2005

Instructions to the Teachers / Parents

1. For the best results, the work in this part should be done in a class room setting, under the full supervision of the teacher or a parent at home.

2. Do only on page or lesson per session without exceeding two sessions per week.

3. The teacher / parent should read aloud each word of the lesson for at least three times, and have the child repeat after him / her each time.

4. Next, the children will be asked to use their favorite colors to trace-color over the two lines of words written in outlined forms; taking into consideration to start the process from right to left and from top to bottom (i.e. the actual direction of the writing process.

5. It might be very helpful, for good writing habits, that the teacher writes each word on the writing board slowly, once or twice, while asking the students to observe his or her hand movements, along with the starting and ending steps.

6. Then, the students should be asked to start copying the words of each page as they appear on the last line, while he or she supervises the writing activity of each student, to ensure that the students do not develop bad writing habits if left unsupervised. Each word should be copied then for four times on the empty lines underneath them.

7. One the writing process is completed by all the students in the class, the teacher should ask each individual student to read the words he / she wrote on the last line of own handwriting; that's- the students will be reading their own writing.

IQRA' Note For Teachers and Parents

Let's Read and Write Arabic (Book I and II) have been part of IQRA' pioneering Comprehensive and Systematic Program of Arabic and Qur'anic Studies since 1993, when it was first published. The complete program is at its final stage; the program for the pre-school / elementary levels has been completed, *Al-Hamdu li-Allah,* and work is almost complete at the junior and senior levels.

IQRA's Program of Arabic and Qur'anic Studies is prepared by scholars and educational experts, and it aims to teach our children and youth Arabic reading, writing, as well as the meaning and understanding of the Qur'an in particular and Arabic literature in general. The adoption of IQRA's complete program, we hope, will lead to a systematic development of our students' skills in understanding Arabic texts and the imbibing of the Qur'anic teachings.

The following books, chart and playing cards within the series have been published since the early 1990's and are currently in wide use in Islamic schools in USA and Canada, and are gaining acceptance throughout the world:

(i) **Sail Through with Arabic Letters;** an alphabet activity book with two sets of charts and two sets of playing cards. They teach the individual Arabic letters through the use of individual words, where (a) each let ter is used in its initial form, and (b) it is illustrated for understanding.

(ii) **Up and Away With Arabic Numbers;** an activity book with a chart, to teach the Arabic numbers with coloring activities.

(iii) **Arabic Letters Activity Book;** an activity and coloring book to com plement and supplement Sail Through With Arabic Letters and the sets of charts and playing cards introduced above.

(iv) **Shapes and Forms of Arabic Letters (Book with a chart);** to teach the Arabic letters and their various shapes and forms in initial, medial and final positions of words. It introduces 84 commonly used Arabic words with illustrations, which can be traced over, colored and written by the learners of the 1st grade and up.

Following the previously mentioned materials, suitable for pre-K to 1st grade, IQRA' developed several other books to continue the Arabic and Qur'anic Program at higher grades of the Elementary Level; these include:

(i) **Let's Read and Write Arabic (Book 1);** an activity book focusing on the pronunciation, writing and meaning of some 250 Qur'anic key words.

(ii) **Let's Read and Write Arabic (Book 2);** an activity book focusing on the

pronunciation, writing and meaning of some extra Qur'anic key words and terms, plus 50 commonly used structures and *Ayat.* This activity book builds on Book 1, but carries the process to a higher level of complexity and contains more working material.

(iii) **IQRA' Arabic Reader, 1 (Textbook and Workbook);** a graded full color illustrated books which introduces the student to modern, systematic and direct method of learning Arabic as a second language. This set of books is suitable for grades 1-2.

(iv) **IQRA' Arabic Reader, 2 (Textbook and Workbook);** a graded full color illustrated textbook with its accompanying workbook, which builds on Reader 1 and carries the students to a higher level of learning Arabic as a second language. This set of books is suitable for grades 3-4.

(v) **IQRA' Arabic Reader, 3 (Textbook and Workbook);** a graded full color illustrated textbook with its accompanying workbook, which builds on Reader 2 and carries the students to a higher level of learning Arabic as a second language. This set of books is suitable for grades 5-6.

(vi) **Short Surahs** (Textbook and Workbook); A classroom text to teach the meaning and message of *Surat-ul-Fatihah* and the last ten **Suwar** of the Qur'an. It provides Arabic text, translation, transliteration, introduction, vocabulary and explanatory notes for each Surah. Suitable for 1st grade students.

(vii) **Juz' Amma for the Classroon 1** (Textbook and Workbook); A classroom text to teach the meaning and message of half of *Juz' 'Amma,* from *Surat-un-Nas* to *Surat-ush-Shams.* It provides Arabic text, translation, transliteration, introduction, vocabulary and explanatory notes for each Surah. Suitable for 2nd and 3rd grades students.

(viii) *Juz' Amma* **for the Classroon 2** (Textbook and Workbook); A class room text to teach the meaning and message of the other half of *Juz' 'Amma,* from *Surat-ul-Balad* to *Surat-un-Naba'.* It provides Arabic text, translation, transliteration, introduction, vocabulary and explanatory notes for each *Surah.* Suitable for 4th and 5th grades students.

(ix) Teachings of the Qur'an (Parts 1, 2 & 3) (Textbooks and Workbooks); this graded level sets of books are suitable for learners of 1st through 6th grades. They follow a thematic approach to teaching the meaning and message of selected *Ayat* from the Qur'an that deal with a variety of important themes.

The IQRA' Program of Arabic and Qur'anic Studies continues at the Junior and Senior levels and most of it has been completed and has been in use and circulation for several years.

LET'S READ AND WRITE ARABIC:

This series of two activity and workbooks, conceived and developed by Fadel Abdallah, IQRA's Research Scholar for Arabic Studies, were first published in 1993. We are re-introducing it now in a new, expanded and enhanced edition. These two activity and workbooks have the underlying aim of bringing the young learners of lower elementary levels (grades 1-3) a step closer to the mastering, the pronunciation, writing and meaning of the Qur'anic language. These two books present key Qur'anic words, terms and phrases, with high frequency of occurrence, as the basis for practicing pronunciation, reading and writing of Arabic.

All of the words and phrases which are introduced in these two activity books are of high frequency in the Qur'an; some of them in variation or derivative forms, occur as many as one hundred times or more.

In brief, these two books serve the purpose:

    (i)   Teaching basic Qur'anic vocabulary.
    (ii)   Teaching simultaneously pronunciation and reading.
    (iii) Teaching simultaneously Arabic script and writing skills.
    (iv) Teaching important Qur'anic terms and terminology.
    (v)   Teachings basic Qur'anic concepts in English.
    (vi) These books provide sure foundation for further studies of Arabic, Qur'anic and Islamic studies.

The teachers must read the introduction and instructions of these two books, not only to get acquainted with the idea and purpose of this series, but also to get specific ideas about approaches and methods for teaching these two books more effectively.

Finally, we need your prayers and support by
(i) joining the ranks of the Ansars of Iqra', (2) becoming a member of IQRA' Book Club.

1st of Jumada I, 1426 / 8th of June 2005

(الكتاب الأوّل)

هيَّا
نقرأ ونكتب
العربيَّة

* * *

إعداد

فضل إبراهيم عبد الله

* * *

مؤسّسة اقرأ الثقافية العالمية

القسم الأوّل .... PART ONE

مراجعة تـــمهيديّة شفويّة للحروف العربية :
أسماؤها وأشكالها ونطقها مع الحركات القصيرة
والطويلة

Preliminary Oral Review of the Arabic Letters:
Their Names,
Their Shapes in Isolation and Within Words,
Their Pronunciation with Short and Long Vowels

Instructions: The teacher will say aloud the names of the Arabic Alphabet and the students will repeat after; then each student will pronounce the names of the letter individually:

ث	ت	ب	ا	ء
ذ	د	خ	ح	ج
ص	ش	س	ز	ر
غ	ع	ظ	ط	ض
م	ل	ك	ق	ف
ي	و	هـ	ن	

Pronouncing the Letters with the Short Vowel *Fathah* / نُطق الحروف مع الفتحة

الدّرس الثاني

Lesson Two

Instructions: The teacher will pronounce aloud each Arabic letter with the _Fathah_ and the students will repeat after; then each student will pronounce the combination individually:

ثَ	سَ	تَ	بَ	آ	أَ	ءَ
ذَ	دَ	خَ	حَ	جَ		
صَ	شَ	سَ	زَ	رَ		
غَ	عَ	ظَ	طَ	ضَ		
مَ	لَ	كَ	قَ	فَ		
يَ	وَ	هَ	نَ			
صَ	غَ	هَ	كَ	يَ		

Pronouncing the / نُطق الحروف مع الضَّمَّة
Letters with the Short Vowel *Dammah*

Instructions: The teacher will pronounce aloud each Arabic letter with the *Dammah* and the students will repeat after; then each student will pronounce the combination individually:

ثُ	تُ	بُ	سُ	أُ	اُ	ءُ
جُ	حُ	خُ	دُ	ذُ		
رُ	زُ	سُ	شُ	صُ		
ضُ	طُ	ظُ	عُ	غُ		
فُ	قُ	كُ	لُ	مُ		
نُ	هُ	هُ	وُ	يُ		
يُ	كُ	هُ	غُ	جُ		

Pronouncing the / أُطق الحروف مع الكسرة
Letters with the Short Vowel *Kasrah*

Instructions: The teacher will pronounce aloud each Arabic letter with the *Kasrah* and the students will repeat after; then each student will pronounce the combination individually:

ثِ	تِ	تِ	بِ	إِ	اِ	ءِ
ذِ	دِ	خِ	حِ	حِ	جِ	
صِ	شِ	سِ	سِ	زِ	رِ	
غِ	عِ	ظِ	طِ	طِ	ضِ	
مِ	لِ	لِ	كِ	قِ	فِ	فِ
يِ	وِ	وِ	هِ	هِ	نِ	
خِ	غِ	هِ	كِ	يِ		

Instructions: The teacher will pronounce aloud each combination of a consonant and the _long vowel_ (ـا / ا)and the students will repeat after; then each student will pronounce the combination individually:

ثَا	تَا	بَا	آ	ءَا
ذَا	دَا	خَا حَا	جَا	
صَا	شَا	سَا	زَا	رَا
غَا	عَا	ظَا	طَا	ضَا
مَا	لاَ / لَا	كَا	قَا	فَا
	يَا	وَا	هَا	نَا

Pronouncing the Letters with the Long Vowel *Alif-Al-Madd*

نُطق الحروف مع ألف المدّ

الدّرس الخامس — Lesson Five

Pronouncing the نُطق الحروف مع واو المدّ / Letters with the Long Vowel *Waw-Al-Madd*

<u>Instructions</u>: The teacher will pronounce aloud each combination of a consonant and the <u>*long vowel*</u> (وُ / وُ) and the students will repeat after; then each student will pronounce the combination individually:

ثُو	تُو	بُو	ـُؤُو ءُو
ذُو	دُو	خُو	حُو	جُو
صُو	شُو	سُو	زُو	رُو
غُو	عُو	ظُو	طُو	ضُو
مُو	لُو	كُو	قُو	فُو
	يُو	وُو	هُو	نُو

Pronouncing the Letters with the Long Vowel *Yaa'-Al-Madd* / نُطق الحروف مع ياء المدّ

الدّرس السّابع

Lesson Seven

Instructions: The teacher will pronounce aloud each combination of a consonant and the _long vowel_ (ـِي اي) and the students will repeat after; then each student will pronounce the combination individually:

ثِي	تِي	بِي	ئِي	إي
ذِي	دِي	خِي	حِي	جِي
صِي	شِي	سِي	زِي	رِي
غِي	عِي	ظِي	طِي	ضِي
مِي	لِي	كِي	قِي	فِي
يِي	وِي	هِي	نِي

٩

أشكال الحروف العربية داخل الكلمات

Shapes of the Arabic Letters within Words   Lesson Eight

Instructions: The teacher will pronounce aloud each word and the students will repeat after, paying attention to the highlighted letter at the beginning, middle and final position of the word; then each student will pronounce the words individually:

عَصَا	كِتَابٌ	اَللهُ ⟸	١
سَمَاءُ	مُؤْمِنٌ	ءَامَنَ ⟸	ء
عِنَبٌ	جَبَلٌ	بَقَرَةٌ ⟸	ب
تَحْتَ	كُتُبٌ	تَابَ ⟸	ت
حَدِيثٌ	مَثْوًى	ثَوَابًا ⟸	ث

ج ⇦	جَمَلٌ	شَجَرًا	يُولِجُ
ح ⇦	حِمَارٍ	صُحُفٌ	صَالِحٍ
خ ⇦	خَلِيفَةً	نَخْلَةِ	نَسْلَخُ
د ⇦	دِينٌ	هُدْهُدُ	سَعِيدِ
ذ ⇦	ذِكْرٌ	عَذَابًا	أَعُوذُ
ر ⇦	رَسُولُ	بُرْهَانٌ	الْقَمَرُ
ز ⇦	زَكَرِيَّا	هُمَزَةٍ	لَمَزَ
س ⇦	سَلَامٌ	مُسْلِمٌ	مَجْلِسُ

خَالِصٌ	مِصْرَ	صِرَاطَ ⇦ ص
بَعْضٍ	يُضِلُّ	ضَلَالًا ⇦ ض
الْخَيْطُ	مَطَرًا	طَيْرٍ ⇦ ط
يُوعَظُ	يَنْظُرُونَ	ظُهْرُ ⇦ ظ
جَامِعٍ	شُعَيْبٌ	عِبْرَةٌ ⇦ ع
صَمْغٌ	الْمَغْرِبِ	غُرَابٌ ⇦ غ
عَفِيفٌ	شَفِيعٌ	فَضْلُ ⇦ ف
خَالِقٌ	يَقْرَأُ	قُرْءَانٌ ⇦ ق

مَــلِك	اَلْكَعْبَةُ	كَلِمَةٌ	ك ⇦
حَبْلٌ	اَلْقَلَمِ	لَحْمًا	ل ⇦
عَلِيمٌ	سَمِيعٌ	مُوسَى	م ⇦
اَلْعَيْنُ	عَنْكَبُوت	نَحْلَةٌ	ن ⇦
وَجْهُ	نَهْرٌ	هِلَالٌ	هـ ⇦
اَللَّهُ	مَوَدَّةٌ	وَعْدُ	و ⇦
الْكُرْسِيّ	طَيِّبًا	يَعْلَمُ	ي ⇦

PART TWO .... القسم الثَّانِي

☺ ☺ ☺

مختارات من المفردات التي تردّدت كثيرًا في القرآن مع معانيها الإنجليزيّة ، كأساس للتدرّب على القراءة والكتابة

Selections of Frequently Used Qur'anic Words with Their English Meanings
As the Basis for Pronunciation and Writing Exercises

* * *

Instructions to the Teachers / Parents

1. For the best results, the work in this part should be done in a classroom setting, under the full supervision of the teacher or a parent at home.
2. Do only on page or lesson per session without exceeding two sessions per week.
3. The teacher / parent should read aloud each word of the lesson for at least three times, and have the child repeat after him / her each time.
4. Next, the children will be asked to use their favorite colors to trace-color over the two lines of words written in outlined forms; taking into consideration to start the process from right to left and from top to bottom (i.e. the actual direction of the writing process.
5. It might be very helpful, for good writing habits, that the teacher writes each word on the writing board slowly, once or twice, while asking the students to observe his or her hand movements, along with the starting and ending steps.
6. Then, the students should be asked to start copying the words of each page as they appear on the last line, while he or she supervises the writing activity of each student, to ensure that the students do not develop bad writing habits if left unsupervised. Each word should be copied then for four times on the empty lines underneath them.
7. Once the writing process is completed by all the students in the class, the teacher should ask each individual student to read the words he / she wrote on the last line of own handwriting; that's- the students will be reading their own writing.

اَلآخِرَةُ * آمَنَ * آمَنَّا * آيَاتٌ

('Aayaatun) * ('Aaminan) * (Aamana) * (Al-'Aakhiratu)

آيَاتٌ * آمَنَّا * آمَنَ * اَلآخِرَةُ

آيَاتٌ * آمَنَّا * آمَنَ * اَلآخِرَةُ

Signs, Verses of Qur'an * Secure * he believed * the Hereafter

والكتابة
Writing

النُّطق
Pronunciation

أَ ـٔ أُ إِ ٱ آ * ئ * ـُو ـِي ـٔاً ءٌ ءٍ

الأَرْض * أُمَّةٍ * أَمِينٌ * أُولَئِك

('Ulaaika) * ('Uammatin) * ('Ameenun) * (Al-'Ardu)

اَلأَرْضُ * أُمَّةٍ * أَمِينٌ * أُولَئِك

اَلأَرْضُ * أُمَّةٌ * أَمِينٌ * أُوْلَئِكَ

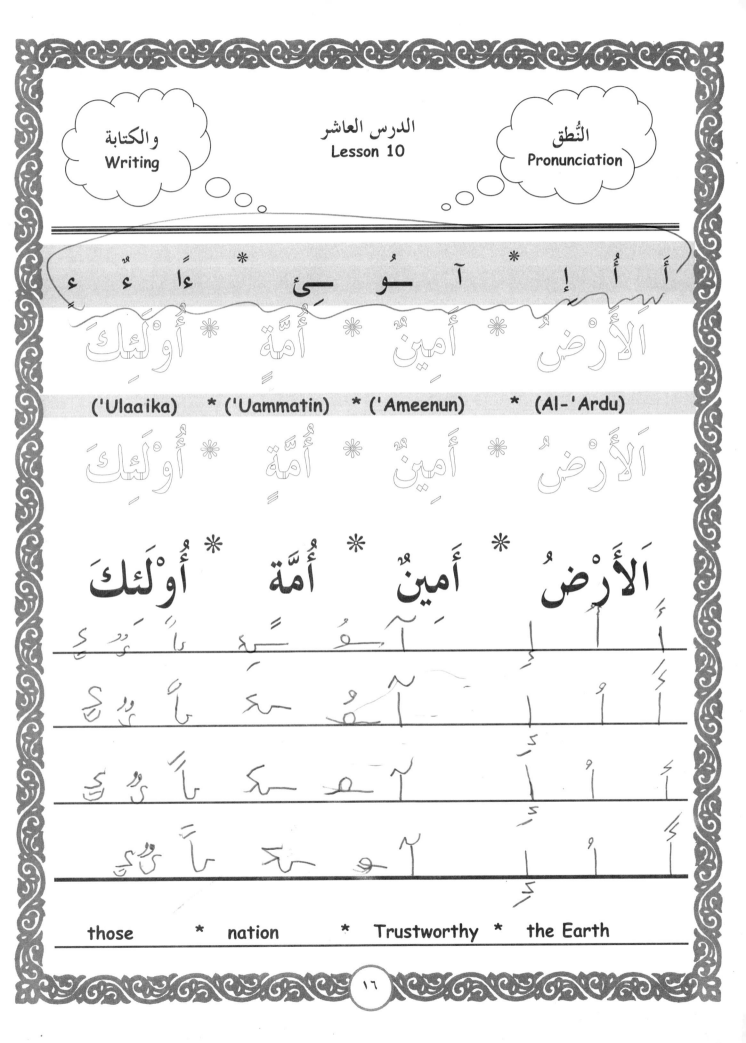

those * nation * Trustworthy * the Earth

والكتابة
Writing

النُّطق
Pronunciation

ب + ا = با

بَ بُ بِ بَا بُو بِي * بَ * بِ بُ *

اَلْبَحْرِ * بَصِيرٌ * بَيْنَهُمْ * اَلْبَيِّنَاتِ

(Al-Bayyinaati) * (Bayna-hum) * (Baseerun) * (Al-Baḥri)

اَلْبَيِّنَاتِ * بَيْنَهُمْ * بَصِيرٌ * اَلْبَحْرِ

اَلْبَيِّنَاتِ * بَيْنَهُمْ * بَصِيرٌ * اَلْبَحْرِ

The proofs * among them * All-Seeing * the sea

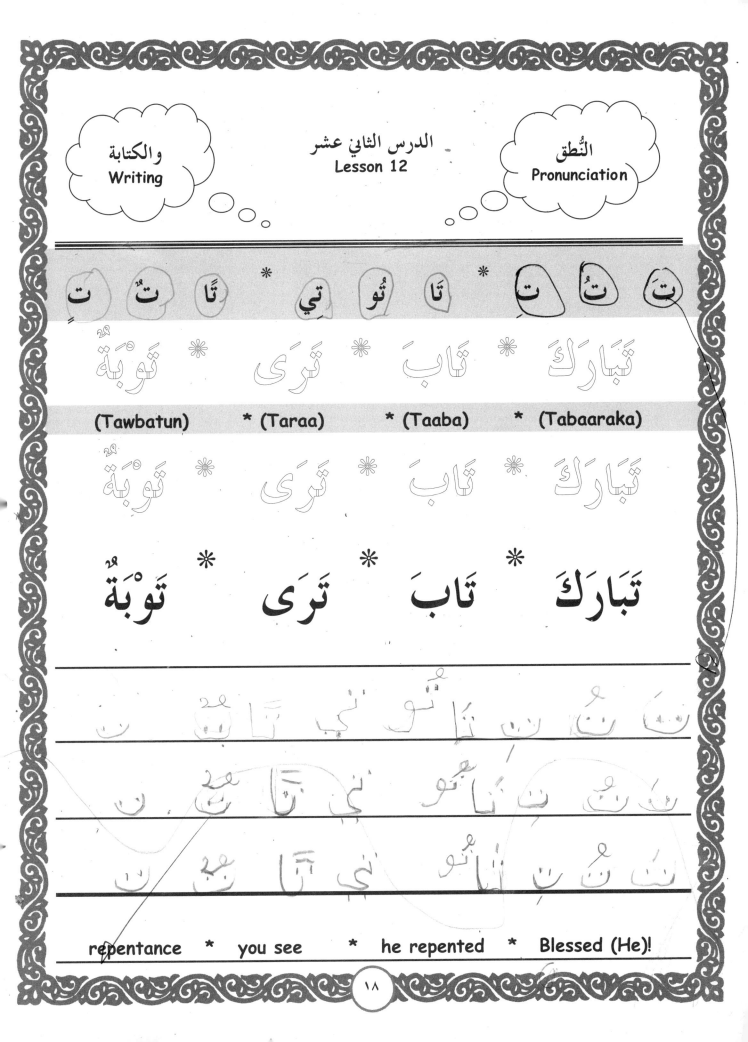

والكتابة Writing	الدرس الثاني عشر Lesson 12	النُّطق Pronunciation

ت ـت تُ تُ ت ت تَا تُو تي تَا ت تُ تَ ت

تَوْبَةٌ تَرَى تَابَ تَبَارَكَ

(Tawbatun) * (Taraa) * (Taaba) * (Tabaaraka)

تَوْبَةٌ تَرَى تَابَ تَبَارَكَ

تَبَارَكَ * تَابَ * تَرَى * تَوْبَةٌ

repentance * you see * he repented * Blessed (He)!

١٨

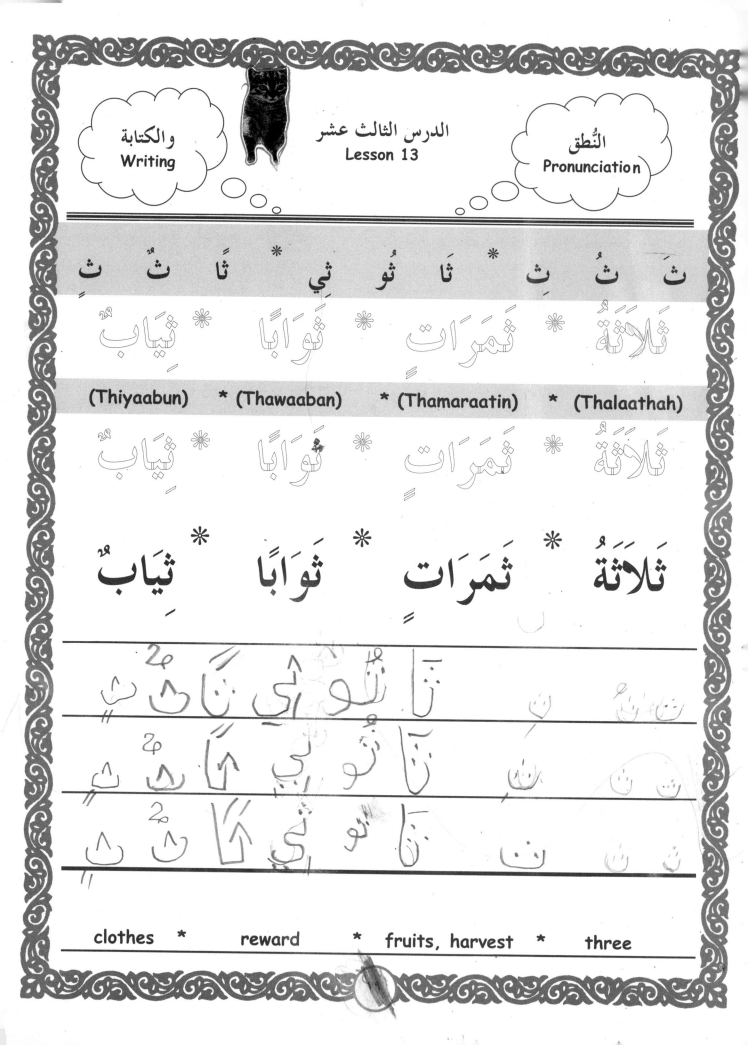

والكتابة
Writing

الدرس الثالث عشر
Lesson 13

النُّطق
Pronunciation

ثَ ثُ ثِ ثْ * ثَ * ثَا ثُو ثِي * ثَ ثُ ثِ

ثِيَابٌ * ثَوَابًا * ثَمَرَاتٍ * ثَلَاثَةٌ

(Thiyaabun) * (Thawaaban) * (Thamaraatin) * (Thalaathah)

ثِيَابٌ * ثَوَابًا * ثَمَرَاتٍ * ثَلَاثَةٌ

ثِيَابٌ * ثَوَابًا * ثَمَرَاتٍ * ثَلَاثَةٌ

clothes * reward * fruits, harvest * three

والكتابة
Writing

الدرس الرابع عشر
Lesson 14

النُّطق
Pronunciation

جِ جُ جَ جَّا جِي جُو جَا جْ جُ جَ

جِبَال * جَاهَدَ * جَنَّات * جَهَنَّم

(Jahannama) * (Jannatin) * (Jaahada) * (Jibaalun)

جِبَال * جَاهَدَ * جَنَّات * جَهَنَّم

جِبَالٌ * جَاهَدَ * جَنَّاتٍ * جَهَنَّم

Hellfire * Gardens * he struggled * mountains

والكتابة
Writing

الدرس الخامس عشر
Lesson 15

النُّطق
Pronunciation

حَ حُ حِ * ح ح حَ حُو حِي حَ حُ حَ حِ

اَلْحَقُّ * حَكِيمٌ * يُحِبُّ * اَلْحَيَاة

(Al-Ḥayaati) * (Yuḥibbu) * (Ḥakeemun) * (Al-Ḥaqqu)

اَلْحَقُّ * حَكِيمٌ * يُحِبُّ * اَلْحَيَاة

اَلْحَيَاة * يُحِبُّ * حَكِيمٌ * اَلْحَقُّ

the life * He loves * he struggled * mountains

والكتابة
Writing

النُّطق
Pronunciation

خَ خُ خِ خَ خُ خِ خَا خُو خِي خِي خَا خُ خِ

خَبِيرٌ ❋ خَلَقْنَا ❋ خَالِدِينَ ❋ خَيْرًا

(Khayran) * (Khaalideena) * (Khalaqnaa) * (Khabeerun)

خَبِيرٌ ❋ خَلَقْنَا ❋ خَالِدِينَ ❋ خَيْرًا

خَبِيرٌ ❋ خَلَقْنَا ❋ خَالِدِينَ ❋ خَيْرًا

good * living forever * We created * Ever-Aware

٢٢

والكتابة
Writing

النُّطق
Pronunciation

دَ دُ دِ * دَا دُو دِي * دِ دُ دَ

دَابَّة * دَرَجَات * دُعَائِي * دِين

(Deeni) * (Du'aa'i) * (Darajaatun) * (Daabbatin)

دِين * دُعَائِي * دَرَجَات * دَابَّة

دَابَّة * دَرَجَاتٌ * دُعَائِي * دِينِ

_____

_____

_____

_____

religion * my supplication * degrees * moving creature

والكتابة
Writing

الدرس الثامن عشر
Lesson 18

النُّطق
Pronunciation

ذَ ذُ ذِ ذِ ذَّ * ذِي ذُو ذَا ذَا ذُ ذَ ذِ

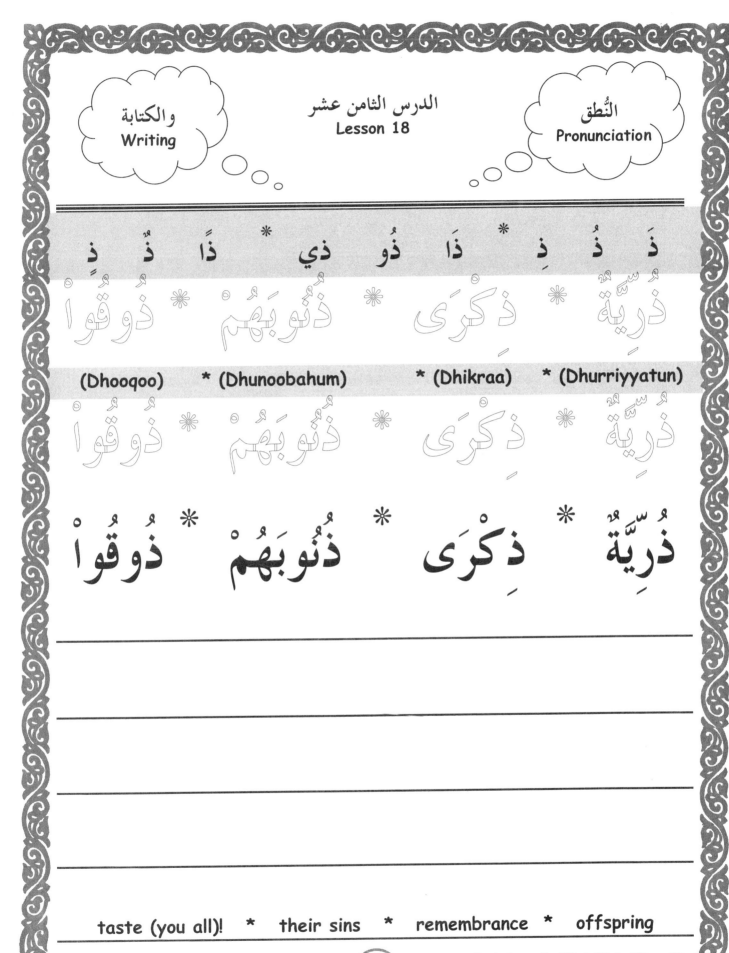

(Dhooqoo) * (Dhunoobahum) * (Dhikraa) * (Dhurriyyatun)

ذُوقُوا * ذُنُوبَهُمْ * ذِكْرَى * ذُرِّيَّةٌ

taste (you all)! * their sins * remembrance * offspring

٢٤

والكتابة
Writing

الدرس التاسع عشر
Lesson 19

النُّطق
Pronunciation

رَ دُ دِ * رُّ دَّ رَا * دَا رِي رُو دَّ رُّ دِ

رَبُّكُمْ * الرَّحْمَنُ * رَحْمَةٍ * رَحِيمًا

(Raheeman) * (Rahmati) * (Ar-Rahmaanu) * (Rabbukum)

رَبُّكُمْ * الرَّحْمَنُ * رَحْمَةٍ * رَحِيمًا

رَبُّكُمْ * الرَّحْمَنُ * رَحْمَةٍ * رَحِيمًا

Merciful * Mercy * The Most-Merciful * your Lord

والكتابة
Writing

الدرس العشرون
Lesson 20

النُّطق
Pronunciation

 زَ   زُ   زِ   زَا * زُ * زِي * زُو * زَا * زِ   زُ * زِ

زَادَهُمْ   زِينَة   زَيْتُونَة   زَوْج

(Zaadahum)   * (Zeenati)   * (Zaytoonatin)   * (Zawjin)

زَادَهُمْ   زِينَة   زَيْتُونَة   زَوْج

زَوْجٍ * زَيْتُونَةٍ * زِينَةَ * زَادَهُمْ

increased them   *   adornment   *   olive tree *   spouse (pair)

الكتابة والكتابة
Writing

النُّطق
Pronunciation

سَ سْ سٌ سٍ * سِي سُو سَا * سَّ سّ سِ

سُبْحَان * سَبِيل * سِبيل * سَلاَمٌ * سَمِيع

(Samee'un) * (Salaamun) * (Sabeeli) * (Subhaana)

سُبْحَان * سَبِيل * سَلاَمٌ * سَمِيع

سَمِيع * سَلاَمٌ * سَبِيل * سُبْحَان

All-Hearing * Peace * path, way * Glorified He!

شَ شُ شِ شَّ شُّ شُّ شِّ شَا شُو شِي شَا شَّ

شَاء * شَيْئًا * شَدِيدٌ * شَهِيدٌ

(Shaheedun) * (Shadeedun) * (Shay'an) * (Shaa'a)

شَاء * شَيْئًا * شَدِيدٌ * شَهِيدٌ

شَاء * شَيْئًا * شَدِيدٌ * شَهِيدٌ

witness * severe, mighty * thing, something * he willed

٢٨

والكتابة
Writing

النُّطق
Pronunciation

صَ صُ صِ صُّ صَّ صِّ صَّا صُو صِي صَّ صِ صُ صَ

صَابِرين * صَدَقَةٌ * صَدُّوا * صَلوةُ ا

(Ṣalaatu)   * (Ṣaddoo)   * (Ṣadaqatun)   * (Ṣabireena)

صَابِرين * صَدَقَةٌ * صَدُّوا * صَلوةُ ا

صَلوةُ * صَدُّوا * صَدَقَةٌ * صَابِرين

---

prayer * they turned away * charity * patient ones

الدرس الرابع والعشرون
Lesson 24

والكتابة
Writing

النُّطق
Pronunciation

ضَ ضُ ضِّ ضِ ضَا ضُو ضِي ضَا ضُّ ضِ

اَلضَّرَّاء ضَل ضَلاَلَةٌ ضَرًّا

(Ḍarran) * (Ḍalaalatun) * (Ḍalla) * (Aḍ-Ḍarra')

اَلضَّرَّاء ضَل ضَلاَلَةٌ ضَرًّا

اَلضَّرَّاء * ضَل * ضَلاَلَةٌ * ضَرًّا

hurt * error, going astray * he strayed * adversity, distress

والكتابة
Writing

النُّطق
Pronunciation

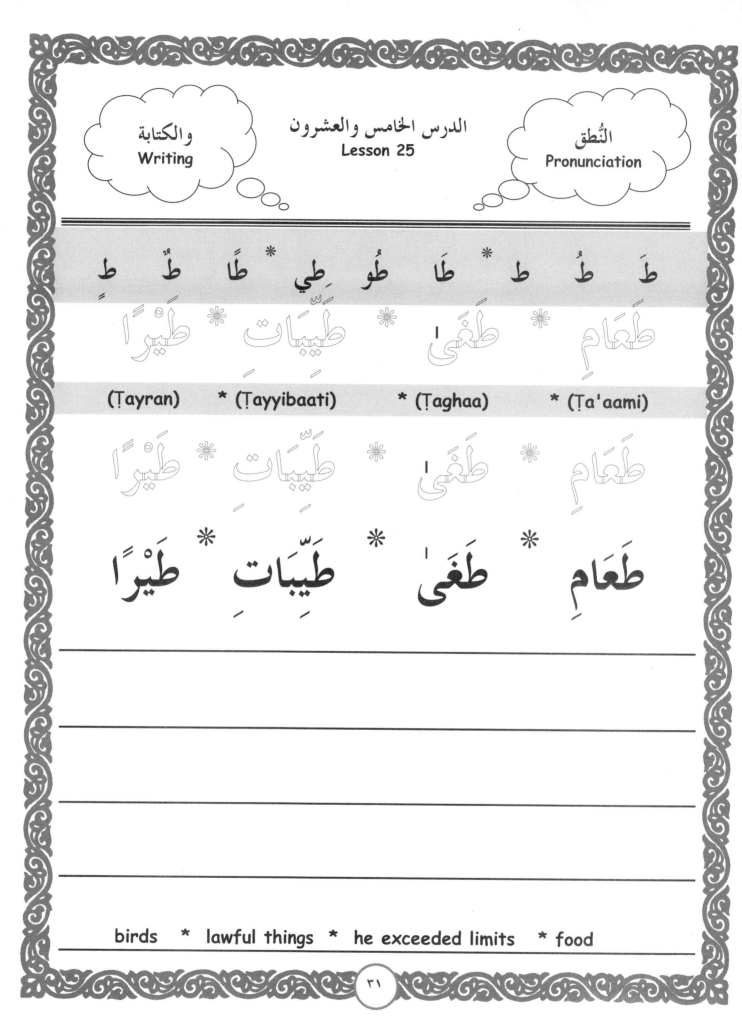

طَ   طُ   طْ   طَا   طُو   طِي   طَّ   طُّ   طِّ

طَعَامِ * طَغَى ا * طَيِّبَات * طَيْرًا

(Ṭayran) * (Ṭayyibaati) * (Ṭaghaa) * (Ṭa'aami)

طَعَامِ * طَغَى ا * طَيِّبَات * طَيْرًا

طَعَامِ * طَغَى ا * طَيِّبَات * طَيْرًا

birds * lawful things * he exceeded limits * food

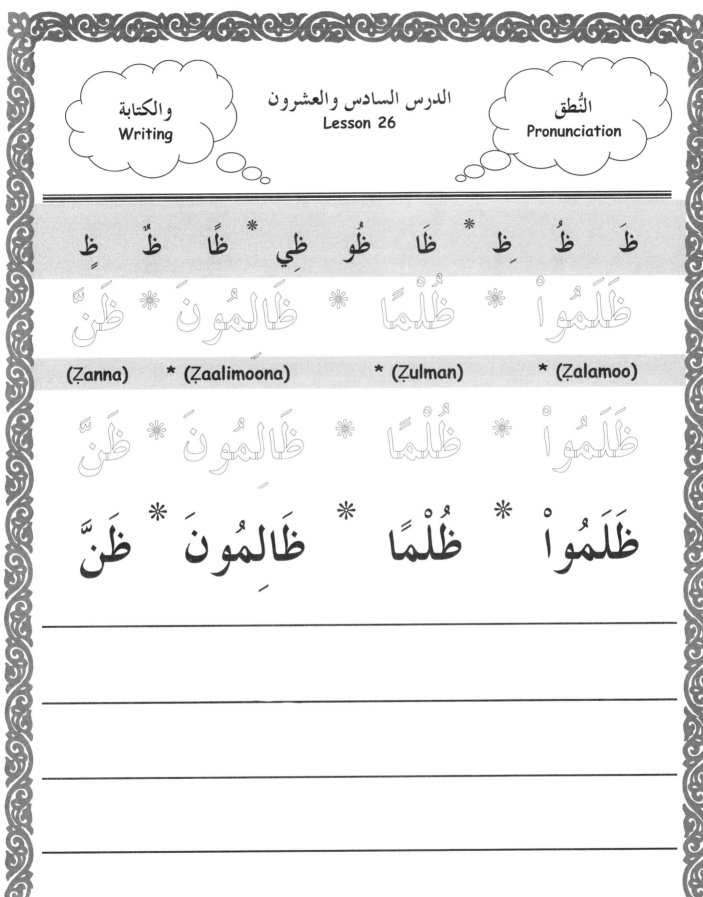

الدرس السادس والعشرون
Lesson 26

والكتابة
Writing

النُّطق
Pronunciation

ظَ   ظُ   ظِ   ظِي   ظُو   ظَا   ظْ   ظّ   ظِ

ظَلَمُوا *   ظُلْمًا *   ظَالِمُونَ *   ظَنَّ

(Z̧anna)   * (Z̧aalimoona)   * (Z̧ulman)   * (Z̧alamoo)

ظَلَمُوا *   ظُلْمًا *   ظَالِمُونَ *   ظَنَّ

ظَلَمُوا *   ظُلْمًا *   ظَالِمُونَ *   ظَنَّ

he thought * wrong doers * wrong doing, injustice * they wronged

٣٢

والكتابة
Writing

النُّطق
Pronunciation

عَ عُ عِ عِ عَّ عُّ عَا عُو عِي عَ عُ عِ

عِبادَه * عَذَابًا * عَظِيمٌ * عَمِلُوا

('Ibaadi-Hi) * ('Adhaaban) * ('Azeemun) * ('Amiloo)

عِبادَه * عَذَابًا * عَظِيمٌ * عَمِلُوا

عِبادَه * عَذَابًا * عَظِيمٌ * عَمِلُوا

they did * Mighty, great * punishment * His servants

والكتابة
Writing

النُّطق
Pronunciation

غَ غُ غِ غْ غَا غُو غِي غَا غِ غْ غِ

غَدًا * غَفُورًا * غَالِبُون * غنِىٌّ

(Ghaniyyun) * (Ghaaliboona) * (Ghafooran) * (Ghadan)

غَدًا * غَفُورًا * غَالِبُون * غنِىٌّ

غنِىٌّ * غَالِبُون * غَفُورًا * غَدًا

rich,
self-sufficient * winners, victorious * Forgiving * tomorrow

٣٤

النُّطق
Pronunciation

والكتابة
Writing

فَ فُ فْ فِ فَ فَا فُو فِي فْ فٌ فَ فٌ فٍ

فِئَةٍ * اَلْفَجْرُ * فَاحِشَةٍ * فُقَرَاءُ

(Fuqaraa'u) * (Faaḥishatin) * (Al-Fajru) * (Fi'atin)

فِئَةٍ * اَلْفَجْرُ * فَاحِشَةٍ * فُقَرَاءُ

فِئَةٍ * اَلْفَجْرُ * فَاحِشَةٍ * فُقَرَاءُ

poor ones * enormity, big sin * the dawn * a group

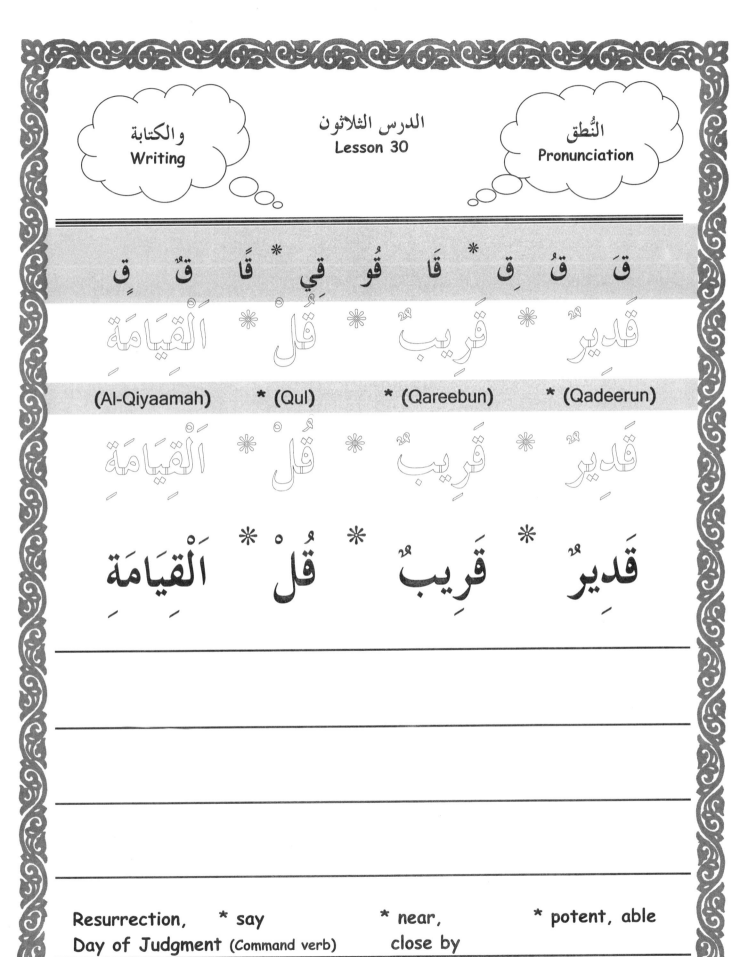

والكتابة
Writing

الدرس الحادي والثلاثون
Lesson 31

النُّطق
Pronunciation

لَكَ لُكَ لِكَ لُك كَا كُو كِي كَّا كُّك لِك

كَفَرُوا كَرِيمٌ كُتِب كَانَ

(Kafaroo) * (Kareemun) * (Kutiba) * (Kaana)

كَفَرُوا كَرِيمٌ كُتِب كَانَ

كَفَرُوا كَرِيمٌ * كُتِب * كَانَ

| they disbelieved | * | noble, generous | * | was prescribed, was mandated | * | was |

والكتابة
Writing

النُّطق
Pronunciation

لَ * لُ * لِ * لُ * لَا / لاَ * لُو لِي * لاَّ * لُّ * لِ

اَللَّيْلِ * لَيْسَ * لُوطٍ * لَعَلَّكُمْ

(Al-Layli) * (Laysa) * (Looṭin) * (La'alla-kum)

اَللَّيْلِ * لَيْسَ * لُوطٍ * لَعَلَّكُمْ

اَلَّيْلِ * لَيْسَ * لُوطٍ * لَعَلَّكُمْ

the night * is not * Lot * so you might
(a Prophet's name)

٣٨

والكتابة
Writing

النُّطق
Pronunciation

مِ مُّ مَا مِي مُو مَا مِ مُ مَ

مثَلُ ✲ مَرْيَمُ ✲ مَعَ ✲ مُوسَى

(Mathalu) * (Maryamu) * (Ma'a) * (Moosa)

مثَلُ ✲ مَرْيَمُ ✲ مَعَ ✲ مُوسَى

مثَلُ ✲ مَرْيَمُ ✲ مَعَ ✲ مُوسَى

example, parable * Mary * with * Moses
(a Prophet's name)

والكتابة
Writing

الدرس الرابع والثلاثون
Lesson 34

النُّطق
Pronunciation

نَ نُ نِ نْ نَا * نُو نِي * نَا نُ نِ نْ نَ

اَلنَّاسُ * اَلنَّبِيُّ * نَذِيرٌ * نَصِيرًا

(Naseeran) * (Nadheerun) * (An-Nabiyyu) * (An-Naasu)

اَلنَّاسُ * اَلنَّبِيُّ * نَذِيرٌ * نَصِيرًا

نَصِيرًا * نَذِيرٌ * اَلنَّبِيُّ * اَلنَّاسُ

---

supporter * Warner * the Prophet * the people, mankind

٤٠

والكتابة
Writing

الدرس الخامس والثلاثون
Lesson 35

النُّطق
Pronunciation

هَ * هُ * هِ * هـ * هَا * هُو * هِي * ـهَا * ـةٌ * ـهُ * ـهِ

اَلْهُدَىٰ * يَهْدِي * هَرُونَ * أَهْلَكْنَا

(Ahlak-Na) * (Haaroona) * (Yahdee) * (Al-Hudaa)

اَلْهُدَىٰ * يَهْدِي * هَرُونَ * أَهْلَكْنَا

أَهْلَكْنَا * هَرُونَ * يَهْدِى * اَلْهُدَى

_____

_____

_____

_____

We destroyed * Aaron * He guides * the guidance
                (name of a Prophet)

والكتابة
Writing

الدرس السادس والثلاثون
Lesson 36

النُّطق
Pronunciation

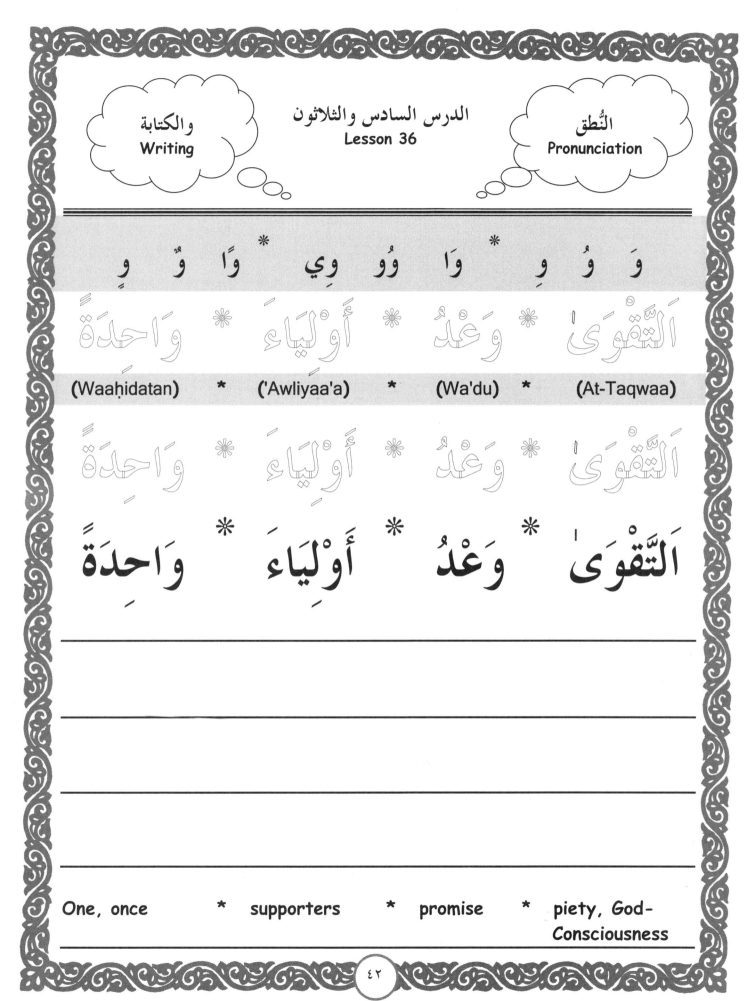

وَ وُ وِ * وَا * وِي وُو * وَ وُ وِ

اَلتَّقْوَىٰ * وَعْدُ * أَوْلِيَاءَ * وَاحِدَةً

(Waaḥidatan) * ('Awliyaa'a) * (Wa'du) * (At-Taqwaa)

اَلتَّقْوَىٰ * وَعْدُ * أَوْلِيَاءَ * وَاحِدَةً

وَاحِدَةً * أَوْلِيَاءَ * وَعْدُ * اَلتَّقْوَىٰ

One, once * supporters * promise * piety, God-Consciousness

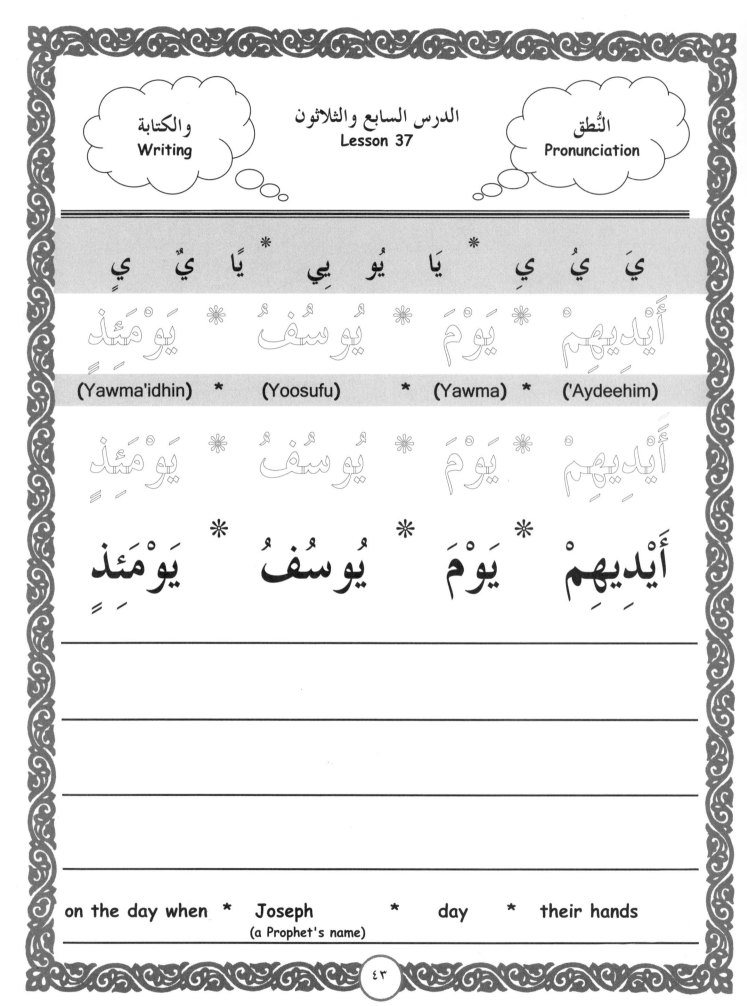

والكتابة Writing

الدرس السابع والثلاثون
Lesson 37

النُّطق Pronunciation

يَ ي يُ ي يَا يُو بِي يٌْ* يًّ* يٍ

أَيْدِيْهِمْ * يُوسُف * يَوْمٌ * أَيْدِيهِمْ

(Yawma'idhin) * (Yoosufu) * (Yawma) * ('Aydeehim)

أَيْدِيهِمْ * يَوْمٌ * يُوسُفُ * يَوْمَئِذٍ

on the day when * Joseph * day * their hands
(a Prophet's name)

٤٣

Appendix 1

Reference Chart of Arabic Letters
With Arrows Showing the Direction of Writing

Appendix 2

Reference Chart of the Different Shapes and Forms of the Arabic Letters

Name of the Letter and Transcription		Isolated Form	Final Letter	Medial Letter	Initial Letter
ألف ’alif **a**		أ	أ	ـأ	أ
باء bā’ **b**		ب	ـب	ـبـ	بـ
تاء tā’ **t**		ت	ـت	ـتـ	تـ
ثاء thā’ **th**		ث	ـث	ـثـ	ثـ
جيم jīm **j**		ج	ـج	ـجـ	جـ
حاء ḥā’ **ḥ**		ح	ـح	ـحـ	حـ
خاء khā’ **kh**		خ	ـخ	ـخـ	خـ
دال dāl **d**		د	ـد	ـد	د
ذال dhāl **dh**		ذ	ـذ	ـذ	ذ
راء rā’ **r**		ر	ـر	ـر	ر

* *In fact, this is a hamzah (ء) and the ’alif (أ) is just a seat for it.*
For more details, see under the Hamzah, pp. 19-20.

Name of the Letter and Transcription			Isolated Form	Final Letter	Medial Letter	Initial Letter
زاي	زاء	zā' zāy z	ز	ـز	ـزـ	ز
سين	sīn s		س	س	ـسـ	سـ
شين	shīn sh		ش	ـش	ـشـ	شـ
صاد	ṣād ṣ		ص	ـص	ـصـ	صـ
ضاد	ḍād ḍ		ض	ـض	ـضـ	ضـ
طاء	ṭā' ṭ		ط	ـط	ـطـ	طـ
ظاء	ẓā' ẓ		ظ	ـظ	ـظـ	ظـ
عين	'ayn '		ع	ـع	ـعـ	عـ
غين	ghayn gh		غ	ـغ	ـغـ	غـ
فاء	fā' f		ف	ـف	ـفـ	فـ

Name of the Letter and Transcription			Isolated Form	Final Letter	Medial Letter	Initial Letter
قاف	qāf	**q**	ق	ـق	ـقـ	قـ
كاف	kāf	**k**	ك	ـك	ـكـ	كـ
لام	lām	**l**	ل	ـل	ـلـ	لـ
ميم	mīm	**m**	م	ـم	ـمـ	مـ
نون	nūn	**n**	ن	ـن	ـنـ	نـ
هاء	hā'	**h**	ه	ـه	ـهـ ـھ	هـ
واو	wāw	**w**	و	ـو	ـو	و
ياء	yā'	**y**	ي	ـي	ـيـ	يـ

Most of the Arabic letters are connectors; that is, that they connect both to a pre-ceding and a following letter. However, there are six letters that do not connect to a following letter, though they connect to preceding letters. Let us call them 'non-connectors', and they are :

Notes:

_____

_____

_____

_____

_____

_____

_____

_____

_____

_____

_____

_____

_____

هذا هو الكتاب الأوّل في سلسلة من كتابين ، ويتبعه الكتاب الثاني .

لكي تتمّ الفائدة ، يُنصح باستعمال الكتاب الثاني بعد الإنتهاء من الكتاب الأوّل!

* * *

This is <u>Book One</u> of a series of two books and it is followed by <u>Book Two</u>.
For best educational results, it is recommended to move on to Book Two after finishing Book One!